Introduction to Teaching with
Webex

M. Jane

Introduction to Teaching with

Webex

A Practical Guide for:

» **Implementing Digital Education Strategies**

» **Creating Engaging Classroom Activities**

» **Building an Effective Online Learning Environment**

ULYSSES PRESS

Published in the United States by:

Ulysses Press

P.O. Box 3440

Berkeley, CA 94703

www.ulyssespress.com

ISBN: 978-1-64604-151-0

Printed in Canada by Marquis Book Printing

10 9 8 7 6 5 4 3 2 1

Acquisitions editor: Ashten Evans

Managing editor: Claire Chun

Editor: Scott Calamar

Proofreader: Renee Rutledge

Front cover and interior design/layout: what!design @ whatweb.com

Cover illustration: © Freud/shutterstock.com

Contents

Part 1

Online Learning

Digital Distance Learning and the Future of Teaching

Whether you teach, parent, or sit in the student's seat, you have undoubtedly encountered the need for digital distance learning. The world is new, and the events of 2020 will forever shape how we view instructional design, curriculum delivery, remote access needs, and virtualization of learning. Teachers prove time and time again that the drive to educate, support, and shape other people into healthy thinkers is the noblest calling, despite the myriad struggles encountered at each political, economic, and social upheaval. Educators soldier on—for the survival and success of our communities. Building lessons, developing and implementing best practices, measuring instruction with equity, and creating classrooms that develop students meaningfully requires skill, experience, and expert craftsmanship.

Master crafters require professional tools, and in an age of socioeconomic shifts, altered classrooms, and dramatically changed public spaces, teachers must be equipped with digital ones.

Digital distance learning, or virtual learning, is the placement of curriculum, lessons, interaction, and materials into a virtual environment. Distance learning falls into two basic camps: *repository* and *interactive.*

1. Repository distance learning models act mostly as a filing cabinet and drop box. They include posting assignments for students to complete and submit, but they offer limited interaction. Assignments are usually edited by the person who assigned them and submitted through the interface without immediate grades other than a notification of "submitted." It then falls to the teacher to organize, grade, and communicate progress. Most repository virtual learning environments are *asynchronous,* which means learning can be engaged whenever and wherever, because nothing is engaged in real time. Videos are prerecorded, assignments are submitted within large time frames, and the environment is generally made for students to engage on their own schedule.

2. Interactive virtual learning environments are more likely to have some *synchronous* and *semi-synchronous* elements. This means that there will be livestreamed videos, discussions that are monitored over shorter periods of time, and live virtual collaborations. This is a more productive environment for learners overall, but it also comes with a heavier workload for parents, support people, students, and teachers, as the interaction requires careful scheduling and management of multiple moving parts. (For instance, hosting a virtual meeting with 19 seven-year-olds comes with unique challenges, as does hosting one with bored or distracted adults.)

Best practice typically dictates that your learning environment has a balance of synchronous and asynchronous elements to mimic in-person teaching. A teacher isn't always performing or interacting—students benefit from having opportunities to apply recently acquired knowledge. Provide guidance for learners on how to apply their synchronous learning to the times they are working independently outside the (virtual) classroom. Digital distance learning means you are providing experiences, instruction, and opportunities for students to apply, wherever they may be.

The future of teaching lies in how we address poverty of *space* and *resources*. A poverty of space occurs when there are more students than we can fit into classrooms, or too few classrooms to accommodate adequate social distancing. A poverty of resources occurs when students and teachers cannot access computers, tablets, or internet connections regularly; when materials cannot be purchased; and when there are too few teachers to accommodate many levels of need within their student populations. Digital distance learning is an incredible mitigating factor for these challenges: it addresses both space and resource deficiencies.

Digital distance learning takes up very little *physical* space. While it does require connectivity and technology for access and engagement, once these barriers are addressed, learning can be diverse, dynamic, and student centered. Students and teachers will of course need a workspace for the development and delivery of digital distance learning, but the classroom space itself is often virtual, cloud-based, and accessible from anywhere. In addition to a variety of interactive resources, digital distance learning makes virtualized curriculum a breeze to embed into online classrooms. Students no longer need to purchase costly and cumbersome textbooks—these can typically be accessed through log-in codes and shared e-book links in a digital environment. Virtual tours of museums, engaging videos, and a plethora of shared (and often free!) resources, and much more, can be housed in a space as small as a computer screen. Connectivity to limitless virtual space dramatically reduces the impact of physical space shortages.

Digital distance learning addresses resource shortages as well. Initially, it may seem cost prohibitive to transition to a robust virtual or hybrid environment, but ultimately, resources that are carefully curated and created will provide learning libraries and curriculum for years to come. Inexpensive devices like Chromebooks are more readily available to students as their price tags diminish; they are becoming as ubiquitous in classrooms now as three-ring binders.

Online Learning for All Grade Levels

Every grade level can incorporate, utilize, and build curriculum and coursework through online learning. For early elementary students, introductory technology skills can be developed alongside curriculum; for mid-elementary and middle school students, more complex and self-directed learning can help develop independent study skills. Students in secondary, post-secondary, and other continuing education programs can also be served effectively with digital distance/online learning. There are similarities across grade levels for implementation of virtual classrooms and online learning, but there are also a number of differences specific to the level of learning.

Establishing a routine is essential for all grade levels. Ensuring that your students, regardless of age or ability, know precisely what to expect in terms of the format and structure will set them up for success; it will also diminish the stress associated with learning a new platform or navigating a new virtual classroom.

For early elementary students, the amount of time spent in synchronous learning should be carefully measured. Students who require help navigating their technology (log ins, website searches, typing) rely largely on support in their home environments. While many virtual classrooms are set up to develop independence in young learners, it is vital to assess the level of technological comfort not only for the students, but for their support systems as well. In multigenerational homes, students will face competition for resources based on the home's hierarchy of needs: parents working remotely may have the primary need for the family computer, and grandma may be an expert in babysitting but have less-than-modern tech skills. The student's home environment, their comfort with and access to technology, and the specific objectives for your class itself are all incredibly important factors to consider when developing virtual learning on any platform.

Think about sending out a technology needs assessment. Using a brief survey, ask your class about their home tech gear and their internet connection and availability. Perhaps you can offer them local resources. Many school districts, cities, and counties provide free and low-cost internet access, as well as options for purchasing computers and other devices. Determine what level of tech will effectively work for your learner's grade level: a tablet may suffice for a second grader, but a high school student should have at minimum a Chromebook for typing, emailing, and researching.

Be prepared to offer more assistance to younger students, English-language learners, students with disabilities, and socioeconomically disadvantaged families. Make sure you are supporting every student's education by adequately using community and district resources—it's more important than ever when you're not seeing your student face-to-face to address issues that prevent engagement.

Many families still consider a desktop computer to be the only way to house information and store files. While middle and high school, community college, and university students may already utilize cloud storage through Google Drive or iCloud, not all learners or their families trust, understand, or have access to such features. Provide, whenever possible, simple video tutorials about how to build and use these free applications, as they will serve students far beyond the school year. Showing students and families how to effectively organize their schoolwork is just as important as showing them how to log into their Webex live classroom session.

Many students are more familiar with platforms like Zoom or Google Meet. Cisco Webex can provide the same features; however, it comes with added security and often higher quality video streaming. More mature learners will easily navigate to and from Webex, but younger or less familiar students may need a brief tutorial on using its features and actively engaging with it.

Younger learners may need help navigating the buttons, features, and elements of Webex; giving them more control (for instance, being in charge of mute and unmute, etc.) is advisable. For students who can more easily navigate, practicing appropriate academic and professional conduct is an excellent learning opportunity. Discuss the ramifications of private chats being accidentally sent out, and while you can still be flexible in your virtual classroom, set specific ground rules for online conduct, noting how to be kind as well as the impact of poor behavior. Consider dividing the class into separate workgroups to maintain order.

Younger learners will be wiggly during live Webex classes. Set the stage for success: Remind students to remain on their seats, with their backs to the chair backs. They should do their best not to wiggle or walk around with their device. Ensure that you have enough time during class to acknowledge and address each student, and tell them clearly what happens if they disrupt the class. While it may seem severe to remove a young learner from the virtual classroom, it is unfair to the rest of the class to divide their attention between learning and disruption. Give clear, kind warnings, and make sure parents are aware of the ground rules and "whys" behind consequences. This will help parents to support your expectations in the virtual classroom. As an example, would you allow a student, during circle time or class discussion, to stand up, walk around, and put an object directly in the face of other students? Certainly not—but that happens frequently when little bodies are at home and not in the classroom. Be prepared to set a standard for students, and to uphold them.

When instructing older students, you will run into the risk of cleverly hidden distractions, like phones. Students will text, scroll social media, make faces, get a snack, and generally behave as they would at home, given the environment. Consider asking them to place their phone in view of the camera and on silent—this alone will significantly reduce distractions. Set the stage for engagement by planning live classes between mealtimes and asking for no snacking during class—this will eliminate potentially off-putting chewing noises and encourage students to be present. Calling on students to respond is another helpful way of engaging older learners—it shows that you are seeing them, you're interested in their thoughts, and you expect their participation. It's also entirely possible that older students will feel bolder in virtual environments—encourage contribution but also be prepared to address off-color, ill-timed, or inappropriate responses. Grading live classes on contribution, attendance, and professionalism creates a standard for engagement that may be necessary to incentivize students to attend and participate. Painfully shy students or those unable to make the sessions may not feel this grading system is fair—you can offer alternatives. For instance, teachers can support more hesitant students by encouraging contributions via written comments that add to the conversation or further its meaning. Recording sessions and then posting the link is another way to encourage students who were unable to attend synchronously to still participate.

Information for Teachers, Parents, and Students

Teachers, parents, and students all contribute equally to a *learning triangle*. Within this triangle occurs the most incredible activities: inspiration and guidance from teachers, support and contextualization from parents, and continued interest and growth from the student. This triangulation is essential for distance learning (for all learning, really!) and cannot be accomplished well without equal contribution from each corner.

Teachers, you are the muses and builders of scaffolding for the dreams of every student you encounter. While you are pressed into tight boxes of uniformity and standardization, it is vital to remember the reason you enrolled in your certification program. It's imperative that you remember what it was like to be standing, wide-eyed, looking up at your favorite teacher as they changed your world with facts, fiction, and opportunities. Whether this teacher was your grandmother, a professor, your third-grade instructor, or your coach, there was a moment when you realized that learning was life-giving. As a teacher you are tasked with that same role: not to teach to a test, but to open children to wonder. Your job, especially when you can't be near your students physically, is to knit together those experiences through a screen, which, if anyone can do, it's *you*.

If you are a part of a public school system, your administration may not have the resources to provide technology to all students; you may be seeking free platforms for instructional delivery, or you may all share a general account for video conferencing. Cisco Webex is an application you can use to create a massive platform for sharing curriculum, ideas, and the burden of distance learning with all of your colleagues. While it works well for staff (this is the Webex "Teams" feature), you can also use these collaborative aspects of it for your virtual classroom in lieu of a comprehensive learning management system (LMS).

Your teammates are more important than ever as you enter into a world of remote tracking and monitoring of progress. Being able to share spreadsheets, curricula, assessment tools, and grading strategies will be key in keeping you (and your students) sane.

Parents, you are the second and equally vital part of learning. While you may not be a certified teacher, or perhaps it's been a while since you cracked a biology textbook, you are still so important in framing how your child sees, interacts with, and succeeds in school. Virtual learning means you *must* support the teacher in their efforts to connect with your child, while still balancing what you know is best for them. Asking a second grader to complete eight hours of online learning will potentially ruin your relationship with them: it's not reasonable, and it's not a reflection of the school day on-site.

Your job is to set the stage for distance learning. Help your child find a space in the house where you can control, to some extent, the background, the distractions, the sounds, and the energy. A corner of the kitchen is fine, but not during meal prep. The living room is great, but not during the evening news. Your insistence that your child's learning is important enough to be given space, quiet, and resources will translate into valued learning for your child.

Students, you are the third and final part of the learning triangle. Your continued interest and application of new skills and ideas is the primary driver for growth and transformation. School is not time ticking away from your life, it is the carefully constructed platform on which you build it. Not everything is fun, not everything is easy, and certainly not everything is fair. Your goal, as a student and as a person embarking on a new stage of life, is to develop something that cannot be taught, imbued, or given: *grit*. You must build within yourself patience for things not easily obtained, courage to reach for things just beyond your grasp, and the fortitude to shoulder through subjects that serve you even if they don't delight you. Your ability to reach your goals and set bigger and more specific ones will be more important than being smart, popular, beautiful, or rich. Evidence shows us time and again that happiness is a by-product of meaning—and meaning comes from actively pursuing goals in your life.

Take this time to make meaning for yourself. Develop that grit. Acknowledge that some things are much more entertaining than others, but prioritize those things by assessing which ones serve you best in moving toward your goals. Identify times when you are most likely to learn well, pinpoint activities that demand your attention but give little back to you, and accept that you will not be productive *all* the time, but that you can be productive *with* your time. Create a schedule. Even if it's written in your little sister's marker on the back of a menu, write the time you'll wake and points in the day you need to complete your tasks. Insert rewards into your day that you can walk away from to continue with your schedule—and place at the end of each day a stopping point when you are not thinking about schoolwork anymore. For example, schedule a walk or a snack after completing half of your tasks for the day. Another reward might be 30 minutes on social media following a large assignment submission.

This is your time to build yourself into a person you admire.

Translating Your Classroom to an Online Platform

Teachers, your classroom is your habitat: it is the world you invite your students into and the environment in which they will grow and thrive with new ideas and concepts. You wouldn't hide a new invention in the dark: you would illuminate all angles, show its functionality, invite participation, and encourage new applications and actions with it. You wouldn't make it inaccessible, either; you would place it in hand's reach of your audience, tell them about it, and encourage their poking, prodding, and examination of the "new thing." The same can be said of online learning! Your curriculum, your projects, your ideas for understanding the world can be translated to learners through a screen with careful, thoughtful construction.

You may feel like your curriculum is set in stone or that, minus your catalog of carefully curated packets, there are too many things you will lose in the virtual world. That's okay! Early primary grades are built on social skills, fine motor development (like careful penmanship and coloring), foundational reading, and numeracy, and these are not forgotten in a virtual environment.

A couple of things are important to remember when creating your class:

> **1.** Virtualization is a *connection,* not a *replacement*. The work necessary to ensure that appropriate neurological pathways are formed through handwriting practice still exists on the other side of a screen: it simply requires creativity and commitment by the teacher, students, and their families. One example is to request a handwritten report, which may seem asinine in an age of texting, typing, voice to text, and video conferencing. (Handwritten documents would be uploaded via email, scan, or through the student's portal in their LMS.) Evidence of correlation between fluid writing and critical thinking can be found in careful penmanship: from improving legibility to boosting self-confidence, the practice of handwriting is an activity that doesn't have to be lost to virtualization. The best way to translate your classroom to an online platform is to think of online learning as a communication tool rather than a teacher. *You* remain the teacher, but your delivery has changed.

2. The key to any well-translated virtual classroom is planning. You can expect this challenge while the class is in development: for every hour of content you develop, students will engage for 30 minutes, and it will take you two hours to develop, deliver, and assess it. As you continue to hone your technological skills and develop that virtual repertoire of curriculum and lessons, you will find those margins to diminish over time—but not initially.

Students, like their teachers, are in environments with different priorities from a traditional, brick-and-mortar classroom. Distractions abound, and for students with any socioeconomic or familial stressors, this becomes increasingly difficult to mitigate. So what's the answer?

Balance. In particular, balance between synchronous and asynchronous learning.

Your classroom has, traditionally, been the place you walk into, own, create, adjust, and live in. Now, you have little control over your students' classrooms—it could be their dorm room, kitchen table, under the staircase, or in a public library. So it's imperative that the virtual space students encounter is *predictable but engaging* and *standardized but personal.*

Predictable virtual classrooms (whether these are based on learning management systems like Google Classroom, Canvas, or others) are ones that provide weekly to-do lists. These are typically captured in modules or conceptual segments of instruction. Navigation of the virtual classroom should be static: students should not have to relearn how to access assignments and quizzes each time they encounter a new classroom. This is important for those live sessions in Webex, as well: students should be expected to access the live sessions at the same time and day each week to avoid scheduling mishaps. Consideration of this time is important as well—are you scheduling it too early for students? Too late for parents? Eight a.m. might sound perfect for a teacher, but to a student out of sync with school schedules, it may be two hours too early. For parents coming home after a late evening at work, after dinner may not be tenable for helping their kids. Asking your class and their support people what time works best for those classroom meetings will help increase buy-in and attendance for those sessions.

There are functional aspects to predictable and engaging environments that you can easily control with Webex Meetings. These include:

- Muting all participants upon entry to avoid distracting background noise.

- Requesting that all students remain seated with only the appropriate level of support from their environment (parents tend to help too much if given the opportunity).

- Creating an agenda that is simple and shareable, with time stamps, to ensure smooth transitions and to address "long talkers" beforehand.

- Establishing entry and exit routines to solidify the beginning and end of the class.

These elements all have specific impacts on engagement; namely, they insist that students are *seen*. Invisible students are much more likely to fall behind because unlike high-performing, noisy, highly social, or even disruptive students, their struggles may go unnoticed. Ensuring that each student feels equally valued will help balance the classroom volume from student to student.

Standardized virtual classrooms are still flexible: standardization of any space—physical or virtual—means creating a solid scaffolding for how individuals navigate the space. This allows students and teachers to build concepts and ideas with one intention: meeting learning objectives for the day.

One way of presenting learning in a standardized way is to use the experiential learning cycle as a framework for each week. The experiential learning cycle includes, with some variation, a cyclical process including a concrete experience, reflective observation, active experimentation, and abstract conceptualization. What does that look like in a weekly virtual learning session?

An experience can be anything *done*. While virtualization increases the likelihood that experiences will be primarily visual, it's important to remember that the learning cycle invites emotion and memory into even visual experiences. For example, if you are teaching a history class about systemic racism, you might assign students to find the location of a historically racially charged event. They would have to do this work themselves—potentially even visit the site physically. You'd then ask them to write a brief paper about the event, with specific questions built around the learning objective. Once students have submitted their papers by the due date, you can use elements of them to further the discussion virtually. Students are given ground rules for communication, and they engage in active experimentation with the concepts presented in each discussion. Following this, students can apply these concepts to current events. Do these things still happen? Do they happen in the same way? What is different now? Then, have them bring their responses to these concepts to a live class session at the end of the week. They will be prepared with their own experiences, have guidance through the discussion board, and be ready to share and apply new concepts at the conclusion of the week.

The standardization is the learning cycle and delivery (research, write, share, discuss), while the flexibility comes from whatever topic you choose. Putting this expectation in place allows the students to be creative in their reflections and explorations, but it also allows teachers to predictably assess submissions and participation.

To effectively translate your classroom to an online platform, follow these steps:

1. Create your big idea for the week. What do you want students to finish the week having mastered, explored, or understood?

2. Create assignments with expected time requirements. These assignments should *always serve the big idea*, or it becomes busy work with no real meaning (and therefore lower engagement). Consider how many are truly necessary to get students to that big idea concretely.

3. Create a to-do list for yourself and your students for the week. Identify how long you believe it will take students to complete assignments, and, at the end of the week, review completion rates and quality.

4. Use the beginning of the week and the end of the week to set up and summarize in your virtual classroom. One to two live meetings, lasting *no more* than an hour, are typically sufficient for K–6 students. Learners in secondary and post-secondary may be able to engage in more frequent live sessions, but maintaining the one-hour window is advisable.

5. Don't assign weekend work. Many students will still do work on the weekends, but leave it available to them for a much-needed rest. Monday should be a fresh start for all.

6. Keep a virtual office hour twice a week. This is a meeting when you are actively in your virtual classroom, but without recording, objectives, or assignments. It's a drop-in hour available to students, parents, and support people. Teachers can also drop in—but prioritize student needs during this time.

7. Keep your grade book accurate and up-to-date each week. When teachers fall behind, students get lost. Ensure that at least two weeks of content is constructed for your virtual classroom ahead of the current week. Let students know what to expect, so they also have something to look forward to.

8. Email is engagement! Encourage students to email you or send you messages about their work or issues they are facing in the class. Use Webex as a place to host question forums and a help desk. You don't have to be on it constantly—but checking in three to four times a day during the week ensures that no one is lost.

Part 2

Using Webex

Frequently Asked Questions about Webex

Is Webex software that I need to install? Webex is an application—often described as cloud based, Webex runs by streaming its service through your device. It is a subscription service, rather than software installed forever on a desktop. It's software in the same way that an application is installed on your phone, though it runs through internet connectivity. It runs on all systems (Android, iPhone, Windows, Mac, etc.).

Is Webex secure? Webex classrooms, Events, Training, and Meetings are run on and protected by a highly secure network. Because Cisco Webex is run on an enterprise scale, delivery of applications is incredibly safe, well supported, and consistently available. Webex security is rigorously validated by independent audits, and the Webex cloud is certified by the Skyhigh CloudTrust Program, one of the top evaluators for cloud security.

Is Cisco Webex a Learning Management System? Webex certainly has features that mimic a classroom: video and voice conferencing, and spaces in which groups can work and share documents, links, and generally collaborate. Webex is best used alongside your own tracking and management systems in order to effectively monitor work, student engagement, and to assign grades. While you can generate discussions and collaborate through Webex Teams and Webex Meetings, you will need to keep an overall grading structure to ensure adequate tracking of students. The parallel to this is a physical classroom with filing cabinets, a whiteboard, computers, and supplies—you'll still need to enter grades in a grade book (digital or physical). Webex is certainly capable of being used as an LMS—it works best integrated into your current one.

Is Cisco Webex accessible through services like Zoom, or do students need to have a subscription? Students must have an email address (typically their school email)—and the teacher enrolls them in their classroom space through Teams. Students will have a log in but will not need to purchase anything to use the spaces. The subscription is paid by institutions, programs, or individual teachers on an annual basis.

Do I have to wait for students to call into a Meeting, or can I schedule them? Both! The difference between a *call in* or *call out* Meeting is that teachers determine when scheduling the class Meeting whether they want to reach out to all students or ask students to join when ready. Typically, it's best to use the "call in" method, as students can choose how they wish to connect (landline, mobile device, computer). You can enable reminders for class time (Reminder Bot!) to ensure students are prepared for their scheduled Meetings.

Can I share files and presentations during a Meeting? Yes! Simply select Share, click the file you want to share in the dialogue box, and it appears on everyone's screens.

Can I record Webex classes and Meetings? Absolutely. The host (you) has the ability to record, and once the session is complete, the file will download to your computer as a Webex Recording file (.wrf). With this, you can choose to save it, upload it to a video-hosting site like YouTube, or share it in your group spaces.

Can I save my recordings? Yes! Even with the free version, you can save your recordings to your computer after they are completed. With the paid version, you can save them directly to your personal Webex site.

Can students access Webex synchronously as well as asynchronously? They certainly can, and should! Asking students to contribute to the space after a live session is a good way to keep the dialogue going. With rules for engagement, it's also nice to allow students to discuss and chat about concepts without you leading them—it gives them the chance to own the space and material a little while digesting what they've just learned. It's also saved in the space like a discussion board, where you can create threads or flag for follow-up later.

Sometimes streaming services get interrupted. Is Webex reliable? Cisco is the industry leader in communication and information technologies: Webex uses the MediaTone Network, making it incredibly reliable. It's still good practice to remember to close other windows you're not using, but it won't affect the fluidity of the session.

Can I change my background or virtual classroom at all? Webex allows you to select your preferred background, augment some items in the foreground, change the style of your Meeting room, and generally personalize each virtual space. You can access these features by selecting your Personal Room icon in your Meeting space and selecting different items in your room for alteration. You can change the name of your room to reflect your classroom as well, by selecting My Webex, Preferences, My Personal Room, and Room Name.

How many people can be in one Meeting? Webex is scalable, which means you can host thousands of people or two people, depending on what services you'd like and how you use them. There are really no limitations on the number of individuals using Webex.

Setting Up Your Online Classroom and Lessons

Whether you are a seasoned primary school teacher or a new high school history instructor, you have some concept of how you'd like your class to operate. There may be Common Core standards you adhere to, specific learning outcomes for a certification program, an industry or institution-specific training checklist, or a broad-strokes idea for what you'd like your students to learn. Whether it's a brick-and-mortar school with hybrid elements or a fully digitized classroom, there are specific steps to simply and efficiently create virtual learning spaces to serve your students and ensure effective and fair assessment of student learning.

A classroom is a living thing: chaos can be expected, but order is essential. Make sure you have a consistent structure, as mentioned in Part 1, that allows students to know what they will encounter when they log in to Cisco Webex. If you are teaching multiple courses with different students in each section, ensure that each class—even if some are using the same materials—has its own unique group space. You are tasked with building community, and students need to know who they are interacting with consistently in order to develop relationships remotely.

While certainly not required, you can integrate and install Cisco Webex into your learning management system. Webex installs in Canvas, Blackboard, Moodle, Brightspace, Schoology, and more through the Cisco Webex Education Connector.

For most learning management systems, you can choose to install Webex into the entire site or into specific courses. You need to be an administrator with both your LMS and Webex to do this.

The steps are essentially the same for all integration and installation of Webex into the LMS.

1. Configure your Cisco Webex site to allow the Webex Education Connector integration. This is done by going to Configuration, choosing Common Site Settings, and then clicking Options.

2. Scroll down and navigate to "lti.educonnector.io" and enter the information requested: this includes your full name, administrator email address, institution, Webex site (your classroom name), and which LMS you wish to install Webex into.

This is the Webex side. To finish the integration, you will need to follow your LMS guidelines for Cisco Webex integration. You can find those up-to-date specifics in your LMS administration guide, online tutorials, and the Cisco Webex customer support site.

Your initial classroom setup checklist should look something like this:

1. Do I have my class roster, inclusive of email addresses and other up-to-date contact information?

2. Have I created a Team or Group for each course I am teaching?

3. Within that Group, have I created a space specific to the course and students?

4. Have I enrolled and invited all of the students, and confirmed they are able to access the space?

Following this, you now can determine the time investments of your course relative to students. How much time is it reasonable to expect students to be engaged in the class? Many students—even seasoned, mature students in graduate school—will find themselves tiring after four hours of engagement interspersed with small breaks. Ask yourself:

1. How much time do I expect students to be learning collaboratively and synchronously?

2. How much time do I expect students to be learning individually and asynchronously?

3. Is it reasonable to expect more than four hours of total work from the students, given their environments, learning needs, and course outcomes?

Remember, all students are different. Your job as a teacher is to identify what the learning outcomes are for the students and to create a target point in which you believe *most* students will fall. If you expect that assignments will take three hours per day for most students, it's fair to assume that some students will finish in two and some will finish in four. Keep a bell curve in mind when assigning work, knowing that if students begin falling well behind, there may be too much content; if they are all completing assignments rapidly, there may be too little challenge in the course. Monitor their contributions by timing assessments, asking how long projects took, and being transparent about how you assign work in the course.

Students will typically fall in the middle of this curve with time to complete assigned work.

Once you've established your expectations and verified that all students have adequate access to the course, you can implement your syllabi or course outlines into the structure of the virtual environment. Typically, modules based on concepts should span around one week in length, depending on the depth and breadth of the materials. There is an apt saying, "experts make the worst teachers," that can become painfully apparent in a virtual classroom. Translation of what comes naturally in a face-to-face environment can feel clunky and odd without the benefit of immediate feedback through raised hands, nodding heads, and murmurs of understanding or confusion. Develop your lessons around a culminating concept for the live sessions, and make it specific to a topic to keep both yourself and students on the same trajectory despite the distance between you.

Prior to beginning your class meeting, create your agenda for the time you'll spend together. Time-stamp each element to keep yourself and the class on track. This can be a simple table, like the one shown on page 27.

Time	Topic	Notes
9:00–9:10 a.m.	Attendance and Welcome, Review of Ground Rules	Ask students to type their name in the chat box to indicate they are present.
9:10–9:20 a.m.	Check In: Two Things	Ask students to state two things that have influenced their week, giving each student thirty seconds or less.
9:20–9:45 a.m.	Question and Answer	Share presentation, reviewing talking points. Begin with class discussion over three primary concepts.
9:45–9:55 a.m.	Review of Opinion Assignment	Share assignments, determine groups, and answer questions about requirements.
9:55–10:00 a.m.	Close Session	Sign off and remain for office hours.
10:00–11:00 a.m.	Open Office Hour	(Stop recording.)

This simple outline for your class session allows for one hour of engagement, increases the amount of time spent in discussion and collaboration, and capitalizes on the togetherness of synchronous learning.

It's tempting to be the focal point of class time during synchronous sessions—but this can be counterintuitive to what you're actually hoping for. Digital distance learning must emphasize flexibility by maximizing what content should be delivered asynchronously—including recorded lectures. Unless you plan to stop frequently for questions and invite discussion during your lectures, you are wasting time in which students could be talking to and learning from one another while in the same space. Recording lectures and soliciting discussion and questions afterward invites students to pay attention to the content in anticipation of the follow-up discussion later.

Allowing office hours directly after your class is an excellent way to encourage students to stick around and ask questions that may have arisen during class time. If students prefer to meet with you privately (for example, if they are struggling in the class or have an issue at home), you can arrange a separate meeting time in which only they are permitted into the class space, to provide confidentiality.

Planning your live sessions is akin to planning a presentation, meeting, or small event. Your live session checklist should include:

- Do I have my agenda, with time stamps?

- Do I have necessary materials already uploaded, opened, and available immediately for the sessions?

- Have I minimized extra windows, closed any personal information (such as social media pages, etc.), and silenced my phone?[1]

- Is my space quiet, free from interruptions and background noise, and do I have note-taking capabilities immediately near me?

To begin your class, you'll log into your Personal Room. Prior to starting your prescheduled Meeting, ensure you are prepared and mindful of the time to allow access to the room around five minutes prior to the class starting. On the bottom of your screen you'll see a floating menu—click the small conversation bubble to show Participants on the right-hand side. This will allow you to see who is already in the Meeting.

Ask all students to use their cameras, if possible, to create more of a classroom environment. You can select different views of speakers on the top right of your screen, including making speaker pictures larger than silent attendees, and a grid view. It's prudent to lay ground rules immediately:

- Please mute yourself unless you are talking to the class.

- Please use your camera, if one is available.

- Please refrain from eating during the Meeting.

- Please remain seated and attentive during class to minimize distractions.

- Please ensure you have all the materials you need for class time nearby.

- Please find a quiet, distraction-free space to engage.

---

1   Keep your phone near you. This may be the only way a student or parent can get ahold of you in a panic with "I've lost the email! How do I get into the Meeting?!" Use your 10 minutes for attendance and ground rules to troubleshoot with those individuals.

- Please silence your phone and place it away from you to avoid the temptation of answering texts and scrolling during class time.

Remember that students will have the ability to chat on the side by default. If you want to assign different privileges, you will need to do the following:

1. Within the class Meeting window, select Participant, Assign Privileges.

2. Then select either one or all students. If you'd like everyone to have the same privileges within the class Meeting, simply assign privileges to all students.

3. If you'd like to remove privileges, select the Communicate tab and determine which ones you'd like to disable. These include everything like the ability to chat, privately chat, share documents, and more. Typically, all students have all privileges in the classroom to allow ease of communication, sharing, and engagement. If you notice students bursting out in laughter and typing, consider disabling private chats. (Or at least worrying students by inferring that all chats are visible to the teacher. They aren't—only chats to everyone are recorded and saved.)

As with all changes in privileges, ensure you select Assign prior to moving on—this saves your settings for the session.

Screen Sharing, Student Grouping, and More Tips and Tricks

Your Spaces are areas meant to be content- and student-specific.

To set up your Space, you will need to log in to your Webex profile. You will do this through Teams, the collaborative element of Webex. If you have the LMS connector, you can access Webex through your LMS as well.

In Teams, you will have your own Personal Room. This is your classroom! Here, you create your Spaces. Imagine that your Spaces are the courses you teach. If you are a primary school teacher, these Spaces may be subject specific. If you are teaching multiple groups of students, such as those in secondary or post-secondary institutions, you may need to create multiple Spaces for each cohort or group of students.

Once in your classroom Space, your options to connect with students appear as icons. This is considered your classroom dashboard.

Your Space is your classroom! In these areas, you can meet, post files, collaborate, and accomplish other tasks.

When you schedule and begin your class meetings, you are able to control and orchestrate the students and their activities through screen sharing, student grouping, and more. Let's go over each of these actions and when/why you'll use them in your classroom.

Screen Sharing

You will use screen sharing when you want to show students your desktop—it's a window that lets them see what you see. Remember—this isn't showing students a file that is open, it's showing them *your entire screen.*

1. Close all windows on your screen, especially social media windows.

2. Consider opening all files (presentations, images, video links) prior to beginning your meeting. This avoids making students wait and watch while you navigate through your files to share your screen.

Your screen share options allow you to decide which screen to share with the class. The uppermost left screen is your current screen.

3. Use your cursor to point to things—it may seem ridiculous, but we often forget that while *we* know what we're referring to, students can't see our fingers pointing to the screen!

4. To share your screen, simply select the Share Screen icon in the floating toolbar at the bottom of your screen. You'll see options for which screen you want to share: the first is your currently opened window. You can select specific items to share, or simply select Screen 1, the general screen share option.

Don't forget to Stop Sharing when you've finished. You can also allow others to share their screens—simply ensure they have screen-sharing capabilities turned on (typically this is a default setting).

Student Grouping

To create groups within your Space, you will assign individuals to Breakout Sessions.

1. In the Session window, select Assign Privileges from the Participant menu.

2. Under Communications, select Breakout Sessions and choose which users you'd like to allow to create breakout groups. As the teacher, you'll always have the privilege, regardless of whether other people do or not.

3. Anyone who begins a breakout session is automatically the presenter for the session.

4. Unfortunately, users who join the classroom through the iOS app or Android can't create breakout sessions, regardless of assigned privileges.

5. Webex Training allows for a huge number of breakout sessions—up to one hundred people per session, and up to one hundred sessions.

When you are creating groups yourself, you can choose to create the groups manually (this is helpful to control for off-topic conversation in student groups as well as creating more targeted groupings for projects, discussions, and more) or automatically.

To create groups manually, you simply select Manually, then:

1. Add a session (there is an Add icon available for this as well).

2. Enter a new name or keep the default name provided.

3. Highlight the Not Assigned participant names and add them with the ">>" button.

4. Select the presenter of the group, and OK.

To create groups automatically, you select Automatically, and then:

1. Select how many breakout sessions/groups.

2. Select how many participants per group.

3. Select OK. The presenter is randomly and automatically assigned.

Webex affords quite a few privileges for teachers in breakout session management. If at any time you need to remove someone from a breakout session, you can select the individual from the Participant menu and choose Expel from Breakout Session.

You can also call participants back from their group sessions by selecting Ask All to Return from the Breakout menu in the Session window.

To end the breakout sessions, simply select End All from the Session window.

If you'd like to create opportunities for students to work in groups, consider assigning spaces to those groups. These can be managed like a topic-specific classroom, and students can be concurrently enrolled into more than one space. To create these group spaces, simply select Add a Space and name it accordingly. Invite/enroll students by email into as many spaces as you'd like. This will allow them to see and interact with people only in their groups. You can also have a default classroom as your general classroom and create groups in their own spaces for their specific tasks.

Archive Spaces you aren't using but want to keep for records or future use.

When you've finished with a Group or Space, you can simply archive it. This is accomplished by selecting the Settings gear icon, and choosing Archive Space.

Quick Tips and Tricks

To get you on your way to providing your classes virtually, the following are a few tips and tricks.

- **Message:** This is the space in which you can create discussions and threads in your classroom. Creating a thread allows students to engage with a specific concept, much like in social media.

- **Meet:** This is the space to have live classes and stream video. Use Meet for face-to-face time with individuals, groups, or your entire class.

- **Whiteboard:** Use this to show computations and other "written" demonstrations in real time, just like a traditional whiteboard or blackboard. You can also use the Whiteboard to play games like virtual Pictionary to get people invested in live classroom sessions.

The Whiteboard feature allows you to draw, paint, and more with students. This can be a fun feature to play with or show processes in problem-solving.

- **Schedule:** Create sessions ahead of time so that students can see what their week and month will look like in your classroom. This will also port into your LMS if you've activated the Education Connector feature of Webex.

- **Files:** This area should remain the repository for all your curricula, materials, and videos. While you may use your own LMS primarily, or perhaps you have a separate tracking and management system altogether, you can certainly still retain files pertinent to your classrooms and groups within the Webex platform. This makes it easier to upload, share, and find important files before, during, and after sessions.

Enter your classroom before other participants. Consider having a "Do Now" posted—a question for students to think about or write a response to as soon as they enter the room. This allows them to be on task immediately upon being present.

End your sessions on time. Using an agenda with a time stamp on each section is crucial, because it lays the groundwork for reminding others there are time restrictions on certain topics. More about this can be found in "Great Expectations (for Student Management)," on page 35.

Clear out unused spaces and enrollees as needed. Reducing the clutter and exponentially increasing alerts and notifications is akin to decluttering your physical classroom space.

Remind students about future meetings with the Remind Bot feature—but don't overwhelm them with messages all the time. Keep updates brief whenever possible and instructions clear and concise at all times.

Remember that Webex has Teams and Meetings: these can be thought of as groups working together asynchronously and synchronously.

Great Expectations (for Student Management)

Even seasoned teachers may find challenges in a virtual environment. Student/learner management typically requires significant guidelines to be laid out prior to interacting with others, just like in brick-and-mortar classrooms. While you can mute, remove, or otherwise easily address overt distractions, it's harder to professionally corral older learners or long, well-meaning talkers.

A few ways to politely interrupt "long talkers" and/or end sessions that are lingering:

- "Apologies, but I'm watching the clock and would like to be respectful of your time. Let's wrap this up, please."

- "These are wonderful ideas and concepts, so let's move them to another venue in the interest of finishing our current tasks."

- "I'd love to hear more about this, so please do follow up with me/us via email if possible."

- "You have put so much thought into this. Can you write these things down for the group, as we have to close?"

- "I'm going to move us on to our next item to ensure we get to each element of our agenda today."

For students who aren't engaged and distract from the group, consider private messaging them with a gentle question about their involvement. "Hey, are you doing okay right now?

I'd love to see you interact more with us about the topic, but you seem a little distracted" is just as effective as standing directly next to disruptive students during their squirrelly times in physical classrooms.

Finally, be *preventative.* Lay out what you expect at every session, and ask for others to support the class by abiding by the rules. Ask students to contribute to rule development so they buy into the process; you might be surprised at how insightful their thoughts are about what makes an effective digital classroom session.

Troubleshooting

The following are some common issues that may arise with Webex, and what you can do about them. Generally, they fall into two areas: technical issues and dealing with distractions.[2]

Technical Issues

No one is joining my Meeting.	• Double-check your URL to ensure you sent the correct address. • Check on the time zone for scheduling. Most of the time, this will automatically adjust in connected calendars, but not always. • Reach out to invitees to verify they have an adequate connection.
My students/invitees are telling me they can't log in.	• Verify the password for the Meeting. • Instruct the participant to close their browser and reopen a new one with the URL. • Ask the participant to click "Open in new window" if their browser prompts them to.

---

2   This section is directly informed by the Cisco Webex help and advice page: https://help.webex.com/en-us/nq0gfqcb/Troubleshoot-Your-Cisco-Webex-Meeting.

The class session is loading too slowly.	• Recommend that the participant log out and log back in again. • Ensure all windows and applications are closed except Webex Meetings. • Ask the participant to clear their web history, cache, and to delete unnecessary or temporary files. • Suggest that the participant attempt to load another page they use regularly to compare load speeds (it may be their connection, which you can't resolve).
A participant just dropped from the call.	• Send the participant a chat or instant message requesting they rejoin—they can click the Audio button and join via phone or the computer audio (VoIP) option.
My browser just crashed.	• Open a new browser window and log back in as soon as possible. • If you can't rejoin on the computer, do so by phone. Typically, phone-in to the Meeting happens for two reasons: the participant has no audio connection for their computer, or they are not next to a device in which to connect. • Consider printing the log-in information, phone access, and your materials in the event this happens.
All I hear is hold music... or weird noises like chewing or people yelling in the background.	• Look at the audio indicator in your Participants panel—the mic will show sound on it to identify who is transmitting the noise. Mute them. • Send the participant a message to let them know about the music, sound, or odd noises. • Remind all participants to mute their line when not talking.
No one can hear anything—or each other.	• Verify that audio connections aren't muted. • Ask participants to check their phone, computer, or VoIP connections. Have them unplug and replug their headphones or microphones. • Try to reset the connection by selecting Mute and Unmute.

Dealing with Distractions

Students are showing up late.	• Continue the meeting and greet the participant when appropriate outside the flow of the meeting. • Send a message to the participant stating, "Our class time is recorded for you—if needed, you can catch up and review it later."
My students are on their phones or multitasking.	• Plan interactions and ask questions throughout to keep students' attention. • Ask that phones be set to the side if it's an ongoing issue. • Mute distracted students and message them to let them know why they have been muted. • Remind the entire group that you are there for a brief amount of time, and to limit distractions whenever possible.
One student or invitee is being difficult or unprofessional.	• Ask that off-topic or inappropriate conversations are taken offline. This can be done through private chat or to everyone in general. • Change that participant's privileges, including muting their audio or removing their ability to chat. • If they continue to detract from the meeting, expel the participant. If they belligerently continue to rejoin, block them.

Part 3

Keeping Students Engaged/Classroom Management

Administering Tests and Quizzes

When considering how to administer tests and quizzes, it's important to establish the intent of the assessments. Are they to determine if students move on to the next concept? To establish participation in activities? To assess mastery in the course content?

For teachers, assessments should ideally fall into three categories in a digital distance learning environment. These should vary in depth and breadth depending on the intent of the evaluation measure. For students, assessments should be clearly outlined to allow preparation—which means planning, planning, planning on the teacher's part.

The first, gentlest method of assessment is a check-in, "do now," or survey. Typically, this measures *attendance,* or at least serves as a virtual check-in for small elements of the course. It could be an acknowledgment of an announcement through email, students simply typing their name in the chat box to show they were present in the live class, or a quick survey that confirms they listened, read, attended, or observed an element of the class. These are typically pass/fail, or complete/incomplete grading measures.

The second level of assessment includes discussion boards, brief multiple-choice quizzes, short essays, and simple question-and-answer formats. Most students are accustomed to these measures, but they still may have some anxiety associated with them.

Finally, the heaviest assessment tool, which has some merit, is the "final" or "semifinal." These tests include higher stakes—often entire modules or courses are summarized in one large, catch-all format in which a variety of question types are administered, and students must complete each section satisfactorily. These types of cumulative knowledge assessments often weigh significantly on the student's overall grade. They can, as a result, lead to increased student anxiety in preparing for and taking the test.

An effective teacher, particularly an online teacher, must weigh the type of assessment with the outcomes they wish to see in their virtual classroom.

So what should you use in your online classroom? If you want to see if students are present, looking at announcements, or simply showing up to the virtual classroom, you can initiate "do nows" or check-ins. These are typically simple surveys, one-question quizzes, email responses, or signing in to note students have been in the digital classroom. When conducting a virtual livestream class, either having students type their name in the chat box or emailing you one sentence about what they learned in the session suffices for showing the student was there, at least for a moment.

For most teachers, midlevel assessments are the most fruitful for virtual environments. Teachers have more control over how questions are asked, and students are not required to recall information from weeks or even months in the past. Midlevel assessments like multiple-choice quizzes, one-page essays, or classroom discussions help students to prepare but not stress at the level of competence expected of them.

High-stakes assessments are sometimes essential for thoroughly appraising student knowledge, but they should be used with compassion for students anxious about performing well in their online classroom. Considering the varied environments students will be in during their testing, it may be inequitable to insist on lengthy, hour-plus assessments requiring sustained attention to detail and a silent test-taking area. Many of these high-stakes tests require proctoring—so in the event a proctored testing site is unavailable, students may be tempted to cheat on tests perceived as critical to passing the course.

To mitigate the use of high-stakes testing, spread out the concepts into weekly modules with a "show what you know" at the end. Consider utilizing multiple-choice tests rather than fill-in-the-blanks to allow students to demonstrate they can choose the right option, rather than testing their memory skills. Your virtual classroom can be a wonderful place to invite rich discussion—asking students to collaborate using the Cisco WebEx Teams feature provides a virtual group space in which students can share concepts, build understanding, and submit group assignments. Asking those students to present as a team builds community—challenging but essential in remote-learning environments— while also allowing you to see their individual contributions, building student confidence in their presentation and communication skills, and showing you what they know. A test that asks what students can remember is a test of memory; an evaluation where students show you what they learned is a learning assessment. Consider also adding question-and-answer sessions to the end of presentations, in which you can further determine their knowledge and skills acquisition within the safety of a group setting. For younger learners, this can look like show-and-tell, an opinion paper, or a story in which they all contribute prior to sharing their creation.

Creating Your Assessments

To create tests and quizzes, you put together, essentially, a poll. You can provide these before, during, and after class sessions to check understanding of concepts at any time.

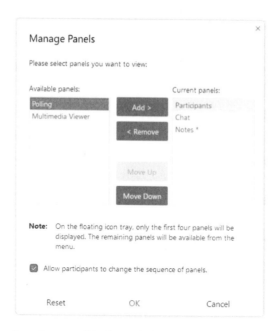

Creating a poll before, during, and after a class helps provide real-time feedback on activities. It can even act as a low-stakes pop quiz.

1. In your icon tray at the bottom right of your screen, select the Polling button. If it's not visible, select the gear icon, go to Manage Panels, and select the Polling button to add it to your icon tray.

2. Add your question, as well as potential answers. You must include at least one potential answer for every poll/test/quiz.

3. Determine your question type (short answer, multiple choice, single answer, etc.) and add the correct choice, if applicable.

4. Select Record Individual Answers to ensure all students' responses are associated with their name, rather than just a standard poll. To create an anonymous poll, don't select Record Individual Answers.

5. Save your quiz/poll.

To select tests and provide them in your classroom, simply follow these steps:

1. Once you've logged in to your Webex site/classroom, select the Training button located near the top of the page.

2. Select Schedule Training.

3. Scroll down to the section labeled Tests, and add a test. You can now select a test from the Test Library.

4. Choose how you want to provide the test to students (either before or after your class session).

5. Choose when you'd like the test to be available and when it's due.

6. Determine the time limit in which your students must complete the test.

7. Determine how many times you'd like the students to take the test.

8. Make sure to check the Scoring and Grading Report box so students' test results will be emailed to them immediately. If you have short-answer, fill-in-the-blank, or essay questions, these will not be autograded and results will not be sent immediately.

9. Make sure you save!

To find scores, you'll need to use the Session Information page.

1. Select Score and Report.

2. Select View and Score from the Student Answers section.

Remember this:

- Fill-in-the-blank scores will be graded, but you still need to check them for accuracy. Students (humans in general) have a knack for answering correctly without exactness—so ensure you're assigning points carefully.

- Manually scored questions can be accessed by navigating to Unscored Questions.

- Select whether an answer is correct or incorrect, and save your updates to the score.

Consider reviewing answers in another class meeting to address frequently missed concepts. Ask students about the test! Determine where the holes are, if any, in their achievement—this helps you become a better teacher and moves testing into the realm of learning rather than scrutiny.

Assigning Homework

If you're teaching in a digital distance learning platform, *all work* seems like homework! Using a *flipped classroom* model can help to create more meaningful engagement during those synchronous times while also providing easy instructions and to-dos for the asynchronous learning times. Flipped classroom models are classrooms designed to provide students with independent learning time (watching videos, listening to recorded lectures, and reading) outside the class (for example, at home or during study hall), for application in the times they are synchronously engaged (live streams, Webex class meetings, live discussions, group work). Flipped instruction means that the time spent together is more significantly generative, as students have come prepared for exploration of topics reviewed and studied prior to class time.

When assigning homework, consider what is best done together (in your live class meeting) and what can be done independently. The lists below show what works well, generally, in each area.

Asynchronous (can be done independently throughout the week):

- Reading

- Videos (lectures or external links)

- Written discussion boards

- Independent assignments (papers, quizzes, etc.)

- High-interest and visually-based presentations

Synchronous (done with the whole class, the teacher, and/or a group):

- Evaluating content in live discussions

- Interactive lectures (anticipate and request interruptions to generate under-standing)

- Proctored assessments

- Oral presentations

- Engaging demonstrations

There are, of course, times and opportunities in which some of these may work better in the other group—but keep in mind that students are more likely to come to class meetings when adequately prepared. Make sure you provide a weekly to-do list to prepare students for the meeting, and again include expectations as the meeting begins.

You can upload links to the classroom Space easily—this is done by opening your Space or classroom and posting files, links, and materials to the class. Students can comment, question, and access all of these items through the shared Space.

You can assign homework by creating a file in your Space with the assignment. Direct students to email you or submit their assignments in the LMS, or ask them to upload their file to the classroom Space. Set due dates, adhere to them, and check in with students regularly through polls and office hours about progress and any barriers they may encounter.

To assign homework, post in your classroom Space what you'd like to see completed, along with a due date and directions for submission. Consider including a short poll that asks, "Did you see this assignment?" so you can manage student acknowledgment of assignments.

Webex integrates with your device's calendar as well as with Outlook 365. You can access this by selecting Settings and then Meeting List.

You can use this feature to integrate your calendars with Webex to help you stay up-to-date, regardless of the calendar you open.

Encourage students to sync their calendars with the classroom calendar to ensure homework assignments can be noted and reminders sent through the calendar of their choice (the one they use most often).

Determining Online Participation

Online participation has rapidly become the hardest measurement that distance learning teachers can extract from their digital classrooms. It is made especially difficult because of the inequity of students' abilities to access synchronous learning. By measuring how often they attend their virtual class meetings, teachers measure attendance and seat time—but this simply isn't possible for students sharing devices, working, reliant on parent or guardian support, or those who live in unpredictable environments. This is why *recording* sessions is so important; it allows students to log in, watch the session later, and absorb the same information as those who were able to attend the livestream. You can provide exit tickets—such as a simple question of "What did you learn from this today?"—that students can then email to you with their response.

As the teacher, it's up to you to determine what should be completed within a specific time frame.

For primary school teachers:

- Provide students with the week's assignments and directions for each one within the assignment itself.

- Provide one or two regularly scheduled live class meetings. More than this is untenable for families, particularly those with working parents and multiple children (who will also have virtual meetings).

- Ask for *a number of assignments* to be completed. Providing choice lets families take a break from tasks that are overwhelming for that week.

- Grade on *engagement*, not accomplishment. If your students are communicating and turning in what you ask (or near it), they are engaged.

- Consider pass/fail or engaged/not engaged as your grading system for younger children.

For secondary school teachers:

- Provide students with an overview of what the course is aiming for. Learning objectives with supporting learning activities for each class helps adolescent learners see the purpose behind the practice.

- Make assignments worth points but use a rubric or labeled scale detailing point values and expectations. If you can't tell a student exactly what you want and then grade accordingly, it will seem you are grading on personal feelings about the student rather than clearly defined expectations.

- Designate the approximate number of minutes or hours that it will take to complete each assignment. Assign no more than a *total* of 20 hours per week of work, knowing that there will be some students who take longer and others who breeze through it.

- Consider a repository of additional assignments for extra credit if desired.[3]

- Provide immediate feedback whenever possible. For quizzes and polls in Webex, make all answers multiple choice to enable immediate grades.

- Consider implementing external websites that link to your classroom or LMS so you can still monitor engagement, despite it being outside your virtual classroom.

---

3   Extra credit is often available only to those who don't need it—highly capable students have the time and energy to do these easily, but struggling students who need it may be unable to complete it. Consider case-by-case extra credit in the form of support—attending office hours may count as a point or two to acknowledge the difficulty and bravery in reaching out for help.

- Set a number of times you expect live participation per week. Once a week is acceptable in times of hardship and should be offered in a variety of settings. Use a poll to determine which times are best for students to log in, and create office hours and live sessions around the most popular three times during the week.

- Consider a scaled system for engagement: 1 through 5 or 1 through 10 for the week, including assignment quality, one synchronous session attended, and communication throughout the week. If you have exams or quizzes or a highly functional LMS (such as Canvas), you can simply create assignments, weigh them according to importance, and assign grades and feedback to students in that venue.

It's important to remember that *seat time* does not equal *engagement.* Students (young and old) can sit in a classroom and hear absolutely nothing that the teacher says—or they can be in the library or at home on their own time, late at night, absorbing everything they can to learn about a topic. Assess their *communication, engagement,* and *learning achievements.* This means changing hats from grading those who *seem* like good students to grading students according to how much they work and contribute to their own learning in a virtual environment.

For post-secondary teachers:

- You likely have an LMS like Canvas, Blackboard, or Moodle. If your institution has guidelines such as seat time, attendance, and submission deadlines, you should incorporate that into your own classroom expectations along with your virtual class expectations. Attendance policies may vary from teacher to teacher or school to school—ensure you are providing students with clear and consistent instructions regarding their interactions in your classroom, even if you need to generate them yourself.

- Create your classroom as a thoroughly planned space that guides learners from "Intro to Your Class" to the completion of specific learning objectives and outcomes. This means creating topic-specific modules, building on prior learning, and encouraging students to pace themselves with regard to their energy.

Introduction to Teaching with **Webex**

- Nontraditional and traditional students alike appreciate consistency in a virtual environment: in grading, structure, and delivery. Every week, list what needs to be accomplished before the next week, laid over the expectations set forth in your syllabus or course description.

- Use materials that interest the students. They are more likely to watch and discuss a TED talk than they are to read through a PowerPoint presentation. If you need to use PowerPoint, give the high-interest talk prior to the presentation to elicit more feedback.

- Encourage accountability without babysitting your learners. Quizzes that ask questions meant to trick or trip up students can create anxiety and be demoralizing. Ask your learners to show what they know, rather than alarming them into paying attention.

- Use your live sessions creatively with more mature learners. Decide whether you want to require the use of cameras. Many returning learners or professionals are not eager to be in a tie or blouse at 7:00 p.m. for a live session when they've just pulled on jammies and poured their wine.

- Assess engagement by how much they contribute—either written or verbal. Provide opportunities for those less inclined to share (shy or nervous students) by using round-robin-style questions in which everyone contributes to the discussion.

- Grading participation through attendance is reasonable for adults—they often have their own device, can communicate about scheduling conflicts, and have enrolled by choice into your class. Requiring them to attend a few live sessions and grading accordingly is a strong way to continue their engagement and minimize lack of participation for the group.

Finally, it's important that *how* you grade is understood *before* you grade. If parents, students, and other support staff or family members don't know what is expected, it will lead to confusion and diminished engagement. Plan your class thoroughly, outline start to finish, and follow your own rules.

Distance Learning and Attention Considerations

As a teacher, parent, student, or friend, you've likely encountered people with executive functioning issues, such as ADHD or ADD. An argument can be made for overdiagnosis or culturally generated attention deficits due to social media and the intensity in which children absorb visual information. However issues of attention may arise, and they *must* be addressed. Environments outside a physical classroom can already serve as a disadvantage for students who struggle with attention: the distractions abound in their homes, on their screens, and in their heads.

Some practical tips for engagement and redirection:

1. Address the issue. State up front that it's hard to pay attention, and ask students if there are ways to help bring them back to the present. This might be a private message sent with a question mark, to be responded with a thumbs-up when the student sees it and returns his or her focus.

2. Target lessons with a clear and engaging topic. Even if you are teaching negative numbers or place values, you can engage students by asking them for input, using funny icons instead of numbers, and using the Whiteboard feature to keep them in real time with computations.

3. Keep the grid-style video on your screen. This helps you to see what your students are doing, if they are up and wandering, or if they are focused on the tasks at hand.

4. Provide stretching breaks. Let students know that they may stand and stretch if it helps them focus on the live class meeting.

5. Give alternative accommodations: ask students if a fidget spinner or exercise ball would help them focus while on the computer, and try to support them in getting those small, helpful items.

Part 4

Activities and Sample Lesson Ideas

Morning Meetings/Closing Circles

Morning meetings create a ritual that is critical for students in K through 6 environments. A morning meeting is simply a regularly scheduled class time in which you set the tone and intention of the day for your class.

Important: While you can certainly take attendance for morning meetings, don't make it a requirement. Invite and encourage students to attend, but daily mandatory meetings are not feasible in distance learning environments.

Consider this: Record your morning meetings to include students sharing their responses to the prompts and to note your intention for the day—but make them available to those children who can't access it at that time. They can still benefit from the meeting.

For younger learners, questions are one of the best ways to generate engagement.

A few questions for morning meetings to start you off right:

- **What will you choose today?** This asks students to think about their choices, what they are capable of, and what their intent is for the day. What will they take agency in? You can provide examples to show the enormous range of responses possible.

   "I choose to be kind!"

   "I choose to be brave today, because I have to go to the doctor."

   "I choose to read my books in the bath today!"

   "I choose to help my mom bake today."

- **What makes you unique?** This question builds community with students, helps celebrate their diverse backgrounds, and encourages students to be themselves without fear. A few examples are always helpful.

   "I am unique because I can roll my tongue."

   "I am unique because I have two moms."

   "I am unique because I have to use medicine to help me breathe."

   "I am unique because I can speak two languages."

- **What is important to you?** This also builds community in a virtual classroom, while also asking students to consider things they are grateful for and what they value. This helps create empathy and set up topical discussions.

"I would never give up my family."

"I would never give up my pet."

"My favorite stuffed animal is really important to me."

"I never want to not have pizza!"

You can choose to ask your students to post a picture of what is important to them to the class space by uploading an image to the conversation, or by sharing their screen. You can also translate this into a show-and-tell activity, in which they can happily hold up their cat in front of their camera to show what is important to them.

For older learners, this can be similar to "do-now" options. Post a question to the Meeting space for students to consider as they log in to the Meeting. Ask them to take five minutes to consider the question or topic, and then create a system for sharing.

- Instruct them to raise their hand in the Participant panel.

- Encourage them to contribute their response to the chat box.

- Ask if anyone would like to share with the group.

- Provide your own answer to help move the meeting along.

Even more mature learners can benefit from creative morning meetings. Ask students to find a piece of paper and draw their response to questions (such as: "What is important to you?"). The more ways you elicit interaction from students during these meetings, the more likely they will stay engaged.

Recording while reading books is also an option—students can attend the live reading or review the recording later. A book read-aloud can be a morning meeting ritual—and for many students who may or may not have an adult reading regularly to them, this can build engagement and literacy levels.

Closing circles are as important as morning meetings. They wrap up the session, encourage students to reflect on the class, and provide direction for the time between classes. Often, these brief 10- to 20-minute sessions are done in three parts: reflection, celebration, and closing.

Reflection: Much like morning meeting rituals, you can ask students questions to consider, such as: "What does tomorrow bring for you, and what can you do to make it positive?" Asking students to consider positive elements in their reflective process sets the stage for celebration.

Questions for Reflection

- What challenge have you met or overcome this week?

- Did you show bravery in anything?

- How could you have helped another person today?

- What was difficult, and what was easy for you during this time?

- Did someone make you happy recently? How?

Celebration: Students are working so hard right now! Alongside parents, grandparents, and other supporters, students are adjusting to virtual learning with teachers, so celebrating your successes together is vital to sustainable classroom practices.

Activities for Celebration:

- Songs—consider a closing song to celebrate being together.

- Jokes—ask students to prepare a joke to share, such as: "What happened when the frog's car broke down? It got *toad!*"

- Big wins—encourage students to say one sentence that was a win for them that week followed by everyone saying "yeah!" at each one.

- Cheers—end each session with a cheer, such as "We might not be at school, but together we're still friends, that's cool!"

- Come up with a closing statement that you repeat. "Take care of yourselves," and the class responds "and each other!"

Growth Mindset Activity

Growth mindset is the belief that learning is transformational—and progress, not perfection, is the goal.

Growth mindset also means being open to and excited for mistakes, because they are opportunities for *growth*, not moments of failure. You can instill a peacefulness about failure in your students by providing lots of opportunities for small, low-stakes failures. Once students know they are safe, they are more likely to take academic risks because the risks are less costly and offer more reward. The antithesis of a growth mindset is a fixed mindset—where it becomes about current ability rather than developmental growth.

One simple way to encourage a growth mindset is to create an activity (this could be a presentation in Webex class meetings through PowerPoint or Slides) in which a statement is read on-screen. The students determine if the statement is a *growth* or *fixed mindset.*

Show each statement on a slide, and when students have answered, ask about their responses and then move the slide to the answer: fixed or growth. Ask students to explain the differences. In this exercise, statements that provide opportunity are growth mindset statements. Statements that are final, terminal, or imply an inability to change are fixed mindset statements. "I can train my brain" means growth is possible. "I won't ever learn how to do this" frames thoughts and feelings as permanent states of mind.

"I'm just not good at math."	"I could try a new approach to this."	"If I don't like what I've completed, I can do it again."	"I already know everything about this."
"If I'm stuck, I can ask for help."	"I won't ever learn how to do this."	"I shouldn't ever make mistakes."	"I can train my brain."
"Progress is more important than perfection."	"I give up."	"I can figure out what I'm missing here."	"I don't need to practice."
"It's not a mistake if I learn from it."	"Hard work isn't as good as just being smart."	"This isn't forever, and I can change it."	"I will just avoid this because it's hard."

Making mistakes commonplace is important in developing a growth mindset. Another activity that inspires a growth mindset is to ask students about mistakes they have previously made. This is sometimes referred to as "the Mistake Game," and it's a powerful reminder that we all err and we can all learn from those mistakes.

You can start off the game by telling about a mistake you have made—keeping self-disclosure appropriate (don't wax poetic on your ex-spouse to your third graders), you can help students understand that even teachers and adults make mistakes, but we keep growing from them.

Consider this: Tell students about a time you procrastinated on a project, and how you had to accept the grade even though it was terrible. Or a time you didn't stand up for a friend who needed help, and how you grew closer when you apologized for it. Whenever someone shares, make sure you elicit the growth and positive elements that came about because of the "mistake."

Building Community and Empathy

Community and empathy in remote environments start with your class ethos. If you regularly state, repeat, and embody togetherness, your class will reflect it. Particularly in times of social upheaval, fear, illness, or economic crises, community and empathy are the critical elements of healing for any individual, group, or society.

Community starts with relationships. Students who are not seen, heard, believed, or valued are students without community. Simply seeing, hearing, believing, and valuing a learner in your classroom can fundamentally change how they exist in both virtual and physical worlds, how they view education, and how they view themselves.

To build community, you must build relationships. This means relationships between students, between yourself and students, and of course, with their families and supporters. Students are already part of personal communities, just like you are in yours. Inviting students and their families to connect through your classroom may seem exhausting or overly intrusive to your processes, but students can't be known without considering their lives outside the classroom.

This is even more apparent for learners in a virtual setting. Asking students and families what barriers or challenges they have at home helps you create an environment they can engage in more readily. A chronically late student in class meetings can either be tardy and penalized, or they can be talked to. They may be waiting for a parent to get home with the computer, or maybe they can't use the internet until they get to the library via the bus.

To build community, start with these two steps:

1. Ask students to complete a technology access survey.

2. Ask students to complete a technology use survey (these can be the same form if desired).

These ensure you know if your students have adequate access to computers, the internet, materials they need to engage in remote learning, and where support may be needed.

Continue with this supportive mindset:

1. Address individual learner needs, like speech-to-text, extended testing times, or additional accommodations for assignment submissions.

Then, ensure you:

1. Create an ethos with your class, for your class. This is like a mission statement—it should guide your class discussions, be the rudder for wayward conversations, and be the rule that governs your activities. Sharing a classroom motto helps you draw students back to the core reason you are there. Examples of this are:

"We gather to learn, to grow, and to care about each other."

"We are here to be together, respectfully, generatively."

"Our class is about building each other up, no matter what."

An enormous function of community building online includes asking students to be seen and heard. This could include:

1. Get-to-know-you posts with photos

2. Morning meetings contextual to learners' lives

3. Discussions that require responses to others

4. Regular one-on-one check-ins with students

5. Partner and group work assignments

In addition to live class meetings, take time to hold office hours with individual students—or host a virtual open house. Create a meeting link for families to join and see the student's work in a presentation or slide show, or to see a prerecorded song, project, or video of the class.

Think back to a time you saw a video and picture montage set to music—from a trip, camp, activity, life event—and think of the feelings it evoked. Pictures and videos of togetherness are powerful and potent indicators of community, and they can be fantastic additions to your class time and virtual environment.

Accountability is another often neglected yet critical element of community. This means following up with students who aren't engaging, addressing live class meeting behaviors like disruption or inattention, and calling on all students to take ownership in the class. This also naturally segues into *student-centered design*, a concept that places the individual student's interests and needs in relation to the materials and learning outcomes.

"Student-centered" means that your learners are the primary drivers for how content is provided, encountered, reflected upon, and retained.

Easily implemented student-centered elements could include:

- Suggesting that students relate classroom content to their culture, family, and lived history

- Allowing students to pick from a list of topics or a menu of assignments that both meet the learning outcomes for the class and are relevant to them

- Asking students what works and doesn't work for them as virtual learners, and then using that information to improve your class time

- Tasking students to take turns being the teacher for a moment, during which they can educate the class (and you) about something they are an expert in. This could be as simple as three minutes talking about isopods or five minutes reviewing their grandma's flauta recipe

- Assigning students to develop your classroom motto or ethos, and creating accountability in the group for upholding it

Remember, building lessons is simply starting with an overarching concept (what's the big idea for this class today?) that is explored through meeting learning objectives with the support of learning activities.

This process can be applied to all ages, abilities, and topics. Here is one example:

What is my big idea?

There is a relationship between homeostasis and the internal environment. Healthy behaviors are essential for long, healthy lives.

What are the learning objectives?

1. Students will explain and describe the relationships between specific internal corporeal systems (organs, tissues, cells).

2. Students will define small systems as part of larger systems.

What learning activities will take place during this lesson?

1. Video 1: *The Human Body*

    a. Guiding questions

    b. Post-video discussion

2. Presentation 1: Digestion, Absorption, Action

    a. Jeopardy! game for vocabulary

3. Video 2: *Healthy and Not-So-Healthy Choices*

    a. Group discussion

    b. Full class debriefing and takeaways

4. Homework assignments

    a. Vocabulary quiz

    b. Systems review

    c. Systems exploration game

    d. Final discussion board posts

This is the outline form of the proposed lesson for learners in the fourth through sixth grades. This lesson plan is designed for a 1.5-hour-long live class meeting, and includes a simplified agenda that doubles as the lesson:

Time	Topic	Materials/Notes
10:00–10:15 a.m.	Morning meeting/Entry routine	Posted question: *What does "healthy" mean to you?*
10:15–10:25 a.m.	Video 1: *The Human Body*	Link in class discussion board
10:25–10:35 a.m.	Discussion	Posted questions: Discussion 1
10:35–10:40 a.m.	Five-minute mini-lecture	Post-discussion (four slides) with summary
10:40–10:55 a.m.	Jeopardy!	Link to game in discussion board
10:55–11:05 a.m.	Video 2: *Choices*	Link in class discussion board
11:05–11:20 a.m.	Breakout group and full class debriefing	Students pre-assigned to breakout sessions (groups of five)
11:20–11:25 a.m.	Review homework for the week	Due before next class Files in the discussion board
11:25–11:30 a.m.	Exit routine: "One Thing"	*What's one thing you'll do this week that is healthy for you?*

Lesson plans can look however you'd like them to. It's important to create a space in your planning that details where you'll find and how you'll share the files to avoid searching while in a live class meeting. The lesson plan below includes all of the elements of the above plan, minus the exact time stamps. It's also leveled for younger learners.

The Digestive System

Outcome: Students will understand what the digestive system is, how it is connected to other parts of the body, and how to predict what might happen when digesting certain foods.

First Grade Science/Health

Five Parts

1. Introduction to the Big Idea:

a. Greet students. Call their attention to the video of the human body, still in the Meeting space.

b. Ask students if they know what the digestive system is. Ask them to remember two things from the video to talk about as a group.

c. Play video of *The Magic School Bus Inside the Human Body*.

d. Invite students to share their two things in a large group discussion.

2. Instructions: Show the Digestive System from Kids' Health (https://kidshealth .org/en/kids/digestive-system.html)

Show the e-book through screen share.

3. Guided Exploration

Pull up a body app on screen share; the $1.99 Amazing Digestive Journey app is interactive, physician informed, and would work wonderfully. Ask students to guess the name of the organ from their list of vocabulary words.

4. Independent Investigation

    a. Instruct students to navigate to their own "What Am I" site. Ask them to spend 10 minutes exploring what each organ does.

    b. Monitor and record student achievements through the linked account to the site.

5. Exit Ticket Wrap-Up

    a. Something new: Ask students to share one new thing they learned during the day's lesson.

    b. Closing circle: class motto. "We're here to learn, explore, and grow."

    Ask students to post in the group chat one thing they will do this week to make healthy food choices.

* * *

There are countless resources available to teachers like you to utilize in your digital distance classroom. Here are a select few:

- **Canvas Commons:** For teachers using Canvas, the Commons are a fantastic resource where you can upload your own content, filter for additional content in specific areas, and download entire courses, individual tests, concept modules, and more into your own course. This is a hugely valuable resource, and it comes with your LMS. Use it!

- **Google Expeditions:** For teachers using Google Classroom, Expeditions has full lesson plans, links, and clearly outlines learning objectives related to common-core standards. The majority of these lessons can span one class to a full week of content, and they are almost always free.

- **Education.com:** This is another fabulous resource for lesson plans, with their strongest content geared to K through 6, but available for other grades. These are free with some limitations.

- **Social media:** One of the greatest resources you have are fellow teachers.

- **Pinterest:** In particular, this can be a treasure trove of lessons shared from other teachers and ready to be implemented in your online classroom.

- **Common Curriculum:** This collaborative, online space allows you to plan from one day to an entire semester easily and virtually. There are also a host of other free resources within it to build up and deepen your virtual classroom.

Your virtual classroom is an extension of *you!* Webex is the vehicle in which you determine how, when, and in what manner your students connect and relate. The more you ask students what is working and show them the big ideas for the day, the more seamless your class times will become.

We're all entering into a new world of digital distance learning; hybrid learning is just around the corner as potentially the most impactful, expanded classroom model to be found.

Happy connecting.

Happy teaching.

Happy students.

About the Author

M. Jane is an educator and writer. She has recently served as a programs ambassador to the US National Office for the Department of Labor to develop distance learning practices that serve underprivileged populations. She has evaluated and developed academic and crisis-mitigating community programs, and taught for a number of years at Western Washington University in Washington State. She holds a master's degree in education and co-leads a residential education and training academy for disadvantaged youth. She is passionate about viewing education as a human service. M. Jane lives in the Pacific Northwest with her two children.